IMAGES OF ENGLAND

BAWTRY, ROSSINGTON, TICKHILL AND WADWORTH

IMAGES OF ENGLAND

BAWTRY, ROSSINGTON, TICKHILL AND WADWORTH

PETER TUFFREY

TEMPUS

For my good friend, Alicia Jordan (née Nobes), sadly missed and will never be forgotten.

Frontispiece: Aerial view of Bawtry with Bawtry Hall to the left.

First published 2007

Tempus Publishing
Cirencester Road, Chalford,
Stroud, Gloucestershire, GL6 8PE
www.tempus-publishing.com

Tempus Publishing is an imprint of NPI Media Group

© Peter Tuffrey, 2007

The right of Peter Tuffrey to be identified as the Author
of this work has been asserted in accordance with the
Copyrights, Designs and Patents Act 1988.

British Library Cataloguing in Publication Data.
A catalogue record for this book is available from the British Library.

ISBN 978 07524 4454 3

Typesetting and origination by NPI Media Group
Printed in Great Britain

Contents

Acknowledgements

I would like to thank the following people for their help: Adrian and Jack Elderkin, Chris Garritt, Mrs Hilton, Ken Kimberley, Karen Lewington, Hugh Parkin, Keith Scott, Dave Smeaton and Roy Venables.

The stationmaster's house at Tickhill; the stationmaster himself can be seen posing outside. The first stationmaster was Mr W. Briggs. After him, Mr C. England occupied the position for thirty years, retiring in 1950. In *Railways in South Yorkshire* (1975), C.T. Goode recalls, 'with the stationmaster at Tickhill were seven other staff who had no colliery about which to worry, the only fuel being that handled by merchants using the yard'.

Introduction

It is over ten years since my book, *Bawtry, Tickhill and Wadworth*, was published. For what may be loosely termed my second volume, I have decided to include Rossington, closely situated near the three other areas in the southern reaches of the Doncaster Metropolitan Borough Council area. I once lived there and I am very pleased that Tempus has invited me back to produce this further glimpse into the past of these four areas.

The pictures are provided by a number of well-known photographers including Edgar Leonard Scrivens (E.L.S.), George Crossland, James Simonton & Son (J.S. & S.), Geoff Warnes and, last but not least, Mathew Henry Stiles. The latter provides perhaps the earliest pictures in the book – two scenes taken around 1900 in the Rossington section and centred in the old, rural estate village. Whilst taking well-composed, pin-sharp pictures, they perhaps betray more than a passing nod to the more celebrated, nationally renowned work of Francis Frith. However, this is in no way intended to belittle Stiles' work which not been properly assessed but has lain for too long unnoticed and unseen in local authority vaults.

George Crossland, a well-known Tickhill dignitary and photographer, perhaps for me steals the show in this book with his marvellous scenes in and around Tickhill. I do not say this lightly, putting him on a pedestal above my postcard hero, Edgar Leonard Scrivens, about whose work I have written so much in the past. The picture of Crossland's that I like best is one entitled, 'Airing the babies'. There is so much character and innocence about this picture and Crossland captures this with his customary clarity and an immaculate sense of composition. It is perhaps comparable with my favourite photograph of his entitled, 'Feeding the Ducks', which appeared in my previous book. Whether to compile another one, dedicated entirely to the bulk of his work, is something I have pondered for a long time.

I cannot help being amused at the number of pictures Crossland took of Tickhill & Wadworth railway station; he must have been obsessed by it. So much so that Scrivens, it is tempting to suggest, conceded the challenge. Normally fascinated by railway stations, Scrivens, to my knowledge, has not taken a single picture of the one at Tickhill.

The trials and tribulations of the station and the South Yorkshire joint railway venture did not go unnoticed by erudite Tickhill scholar, the late Tom Beastall, in his book, *Tickhill, Portrait of an English Country Town*. He couldn't help but get himself involved in recounting its troubled history. So too C.T. Goode, who seems bemused by the whole undertaking in his admirable book, *South Yorkshire Railways*. Another friend and former colleague, Geoff Warnes, along with his chum Don Temporal, provides unique views of the East Coast mainline at Rossington and around the station. A book of Geoff Warnes' work is perhaps also long overdue.

For much of the information about Crossland and Tickhill itself, I am indebted to my good friend Ken Kimberley — a fountain of knowledge and tireless collector of the images of the area. Another friend, Tom Beastall, provided me with additional information prior to his untimely death. Indeed, our forays through the archives at Sandbeck and leg-pulling with Lord Scarborough ('Bo Bo' to his friends) were very enjoyable times indeed.

Crossland, unfortunately, never seems to have taken his camera out of the Tickhill area. By contrast, Scrivens is present in Bawtry, Rossington and Tickhill, making his mark very prominently. The breadth and variety of his work is sometimes breathtaking. He feels comfortable and inspired whether capturing a hunt meet (at Bawtry or Rossington), cutting the first sod for a colliery (at Rossington) or wandering round a newly laid-out model colliery village (at Rossington).

Some of the pictures of Tickhill, which Scrivens claims to be his own, may be the work of Crossland or another, as yet undocumented photographer, Thomas Clixby. A closer look at some of Scrivens' photographs reveals the tell-tale signs — unsuccessful attempts to completely obliterate the titling on views not taken by him but subsequently reprinted bearing his initials. This has been detected not only in Tickhill views but also on cards of other areas. Whether Scrivens bought the views under license or paid for the copyright is unclear. Sadly this information, along with whatever collaboration he had with Crossland, is now perhaps lost forever.

Scrivens is conspicuous by his absence in Wadworth: not so with his rivals, the Balby-based James Simonton & Son. Admittedly, father and son were not so energetic as Scrivens, capturing local scenes and events within a 50-mile radius of Doncaster with amazing stamina. Yet it cannot be denied they have recorded a sleepy, rustic and rural Wadworth prior to the massive redevelopments which took place there during the 1960s and '70s. After viewing these images, it is impossible not to take time to reflect — was it all for the good? Admittedly the properties were torn down due to unsanitary conditions, but would they have suffered the same fate today under the rigorous constraints of conservation which hold developers in abeyance today? We can only wonder. In the meantime, it cannot be denied that Wadworth has had its heart torn out. The same is not true of Bawtry and Tickhill, largely because both areas escaped industrial development, whilst housing seems not to have imposed too drastically on the core of the settlement, though it cannot be denied that some infilling of the main thoroughfares has been insensitive.

Rossington's old village atmosphere on the east side of the East Coast mainline has long been obliterated by modern housing developments. The west side of the course of the railway line was taken by the Colliery Company for housing etc. How the whole area will respond to the closure of the colliery will no doubt unfold in time. Finally, I dedicate this book to Alicia Jordan (née Nobes), my good friend at Doncaster Art College (1970-1971) and former Tickhill resident who enlightened me on the area's charm whilst I was living in Rossington.

one

Rambling
Round

Church Street, Bawtry, looking east towards St Nicholas's church. In the pamphlet, *Bawtry Hall, a brief history from information supplied by Leslie Smith,* it is stated:

> The small market town of Bawtry was created by Idonea Viponts in the twelfth century. For hundreds of years it stood on the Great North Road, the main route from London to the North... In medieval times it was the place of assembly for the sheriff, archbishop, officers of the crown and their retinues whenever members of the royal family travelled North into Yorkshire... The original North Road ran along Top Lane, through what is now the main gate of the RAF headquarters and on into the grounds... Before the present hall was built the road was diverted into the Market Place of Bawtry and now runs to the east of the hall.

Gainsborough Road, looking south with the Ship Inn dominating the centre of the picture. Bawtry lies at a point where the Great North Road crosses the river Idle. It is located in the Metropolitan Borough of Doncaster (part of South Yorkshire), on the border with Nottinghamshire and between Bircotes and Misson, on the junction of the A514, A631 and A63 roads.

Above: Church Street by Doncaster-based photographers, James Simonton & Son. Note the premises of a joiner and decorator on the right. Bawtry once possessed a number of yards and alleys extending from its main streets. Most have disappeared today and many of them ran off Low Street and Church Street. They included Fielding's Row, Chapel Row, Church Lane, Pearson's Row and Birley's Yard.

Below: The south side of High Street, Bawtry, looking towards the Marquis of Granby public house, by Doncaster-based photographer, Edgar Leonard Scrivens. As he began producing postcard views, all bearing his initials E.L.S., he evolved a meticulous numbering system. For example, on a card numbered 2-20, the first digit refers to the locality; in this case, the number '2' relates to Bawtry. The second number indicates the postcard is the twentieth in the Bawtry series. Scrivens photographed over 250 localities with a fair number of cards in each series. In the 1920s and '30s, he re-photographed a number of areas recorded earlier in his career, adding the letter 'G' or 'V' depending on the period, to the numbering of the cards.

High Street, Bawtry, featuring the premises of Herring and Glasbey grocers and provision dealers. A. Herring, grocer of Bawtry, died suddenly on 23 March 1934 at the age of sixty-eight. He was born in Cornwall, though had been in Bawtry for around thirty years. In his early years in Bawtry he was with H. J. Willows, grocer, then in partnership with a Mr Glasbey, and when the First World War came, he started in business in Bawtry High Street. He was a keen musician and in his early days was a singer and cellist. He had been choirmaster for a number of years at Bawtry Wesleyan Chapel, was society steward, a trustee of the Methodist church, and a leader of the Bible class.

Aerial view of Bawtry with High Street and St Nicholas's church in the top half of the picture.

View of the north side of High Street that includes H. Hoyes' business premises – the building dating from 1691 being erected by the Dawson family. The Town Hall is the fine structure adjacent, built in 1890.

Market Place, Bawtry, with the premises of the Bawtry Motor Co. on the right. John Thomas Walker started the business around 1900, dealing in cycles, then motorcycles and later motor cars. He sold the business in 1946. The house on the left adjacent to the Crown Hotel (out of view) was built around 1800 and the bays added in the late nineteenth century.

Bawtry's South Parade, looking south-west. Featured on the left is the Palace Cinema. Local saddler Tom Frost acquired the site for the venture in 1913 but it did not open until the time of the First World War, 1914-18. After some initial failures, Ron Curry, in *Let's Go to the Pictures* (n.d.), notes: 'Ken Simpkins took out a ten-year lease in the 1920s and the Palace became a success... Towards the end of the [Second World] War, the lease was due to expire and Mr Simpkins purchased the freehold'. Around 1951 the business was sold to a Mr Eckhard of the Three Star Cinemas. Later owners included the Marshalls, who subsequently developed the site as a garage. The Palace closed in the early 1960s.

Another view of South Parade, looking south-west with part of the perimeter wall to Bawtry Hall on the right. After the Turnpike Act of 1759, Britain's roads improved and stagecoaches ran regular services from stage to stage. Bawtry was one of these stages. And it might be argued that South Parade must have made a favourable impression on visitors entering from the south as it contained quite a number of large houses.

Station Road, Bawtry, looking towards the stationmaster's house, built 1848-49 by the Great Northern Railway Co. In general, the coming of the railway did not kill road transport, as many minor roads and their traffic became important feeder services for the railways. Building work for many of the houses in Station Road – of which there are some impressive examples – took place after the coming of the railways. The history of transport in Bawtry is one of progression from river to road, from road to rail and, finally, from rail back to road, not forgetting the new facilities provided by the opening of the nearby Robin Hood Airport.

Tickhill Road, Bawtry, with High Street in the distance. Bawtry is now largely a dormitory town with many people working out of the area, taking advantage of the convenient road systems nearby.

Rossington Bridge, facing south. There are remains of both a Roman fort and Roman pottery kilns in the Rossington area. During the late nineteenth century, Rossington was described as a small village situated on the south side of the river Torne, which is crossed by several bridges.

> The surface is of a hilly nature and the land is fertile, with a soil of sand, gravel and clay, and subsoil of the same… The manor was, for a long period, the seat of the Fossard and Mauley families and was granted by Henry VII to the Corporation of Doncaster, from whom it was purchased by the late J. Brown of Harehills Grove near Leeds in 1838.

Rossington Bridge, facing north. The buildings on the left have since been demolished. Rossington is a former mining village to the south-east of Doncaster. The property on the right was an inn until the mid-nineteenth century. The house recently reverted back to its former use, becoming known as the Hare and Tortoise. The area is known informally as 'Parrot's Corner', though the origin of this name is uncertain. Rossington Bridge is its more formal name.

Above: Foljambe Crescent, Rossington (to the left), from King George's Road. During the early twentieth century, there was considerable expansion in the Rossington area. The need for workers in and around the colliery led to the building of large numbers of houses near to the pit in what was called 'New Rossington'.

Below: Allenby Crescent, New Rossington, taken by Edgar Leonard Scrivens. The first sod at the colliery was cut on 10 June 1912 and the first coal brought up three years later. One of Allenby Crescent's occupants, May Shaw, remembers the following about the early days:

> The street was full of characters like Mr Moore, the father of George Moore, who used to make pop and sell it on Sundays. Mr Pagan, who lived next door to me and made wonderful furniture… Mrs Cleaver made pie and peas every Tuesday and Friday. Mrs Bastie made cobs of bread, Mrs Hatton used to run a sweet shop. Mr Finney used to charge accumulators and batteries for wireless sets and Mrs Sharrot ran money clubs for clothes at a cost of 6d per week.

Above: Central Drive, Rossington. By 1917, coal production was well on its way and Rossington's population grew from 342 in 1901 to 3,026 in 1916. By 1935 the pit was employing around 3,000 men and boys.

Below: Fowler Crescent, New Rossington. In an article printed by the *Doncaster Gazette*, dated 1 August 1913 and entitled 'Colliers' Village on the Way', it is stated that:

> The pastoral calm that has brooded for so long over the woods and meadows around Rossington is already giving place to the bustle and hustle that come in the wake of colliery enterprise.
>
> The Rossington colliery village which is now coming into being occupies a charming situation, surrounded by trees on nearly every side and completely screened from the colliery itself by a deep wood. The site, which is about three-quarters of a mile from the old village, extends from Grange Lane on one side to West End Lane on the other and both these lanes are being straightened and made into good 40-feet roads.

Grantham Road, New Rossington. Further information from the *Gazette* article of 1 August 1913 reads:

> The boundaries of the village make an irregular four-sided figure, but the greater part of the houses are planned in perfect concentric circles as the New Village at Maltby. The inner circle consists of the official houses, these being semi-detached villas facing a central park. The second circle is formed of workmen's houses of a superior type and the third and outermost circle of somewhat smaller houses, both of these being set in blocks of from four to ten houses each. Outside this circular formation there are streets of houses running at a tangent on the west and east sides respectively and there are also fifty houses with a frontage to West End Lane. The building line of all the houses is more or less curved and they all have lawns and asphalt paths in front, and asphalt yards and gardens behind. Moreover, all the streets are made to a width of 48 feet, including those which run right through the centre of the village, from north to south and from east to west while the back roads are 15 feet wide, so that there will be ample air space for the dwellers in this latest model village.

King George Road, New Rossington. The *Doncaster Gazette* of 1 August informs readers that, 'altogether, some 840 houses are to be erected on this site [Rossington's New Village] and it may be mentioned that Mr Streatfield [the Squire of Rossington] has definitely placed a ban on speculative building on any other part of his estate, so that the colliery workers will always form a separate and self-contained community'.

A view of Rossington looking towards St Michael's church, taken by Edgar Leonard Scrivens, *c.* 1925.

Station Road, Rossington in the snow, looking towards the railway station. On the left is a Victorian pump. In his work, *Rossington: Glimpses into the Past* (1986), Frank Clarke describes this pump:

> Said to be built of Roche Abbey [near Maltby] stone and dating from about 1850. It is unique to the Doncaster area. In 1924 R.J. Streatfield supplied drinking cups at the request of the parish council. In 1957 there was a public outcry when plans were put forward to demolish the pump. It was reprieved when Mr Percy Smith discovered that it stood on land purchased by him in 1939.

Station Road, Rossington, looking south-east towards the church. The building on the left is Ivy House Farm.

A scene from outside St Michael's church, Rossington. This picture was taken by Matthew Henry Stiles. Interestingly, an 1871 trade directory states:

> The church was entirely rebuilt in 1844 and is an elegant structure in the early English style, comprising nave, chancel, north and south transepts, small south porch and tower. The chancel arch is a splendid specimen of Norman architecture, finely carved and in good preservation. The south doorway is also Norman and both it and the arch were replaced with great care at the restoration of the church. The east window consists of one large light, filled with rich stained glass, representing St Michael and the Dragon, executed by J.B. Cappronier of Brussels. In the chancel is a marble tablet to the memory of James Brown, Esq. of Harehills Grove, near Leeds, who died in 1845, and at whose sole expense the church was rebuilt.

York Street, New Rossington, captured by Edgar Leonard Scrivens. Local resident Bill Winfield recounts the days when families moved from the North East to Rossington so they could find work at the pit:

> As many of these early settlers were from Durham and Northumberland it was only natural that they be housed together. Socially and culturally they had a lot in common, especially lingo-wise. Holmes Carr Road and the Crescent were allotted to many of these families, so it comes as no surprise that it became known as 'Geordie Land'. Sometime later, a large influx came from Lancashire and they were housed in Aberconway, Central Drive, Haigh Crescent, Junction Road etc., which immediately became known as 'Little Wigan'.

Station Road, Rossington, with Stripe Road leading off to the left. Before the sinking of the pit, farming was the major industry in Rossington, although a brick works was in operation in the late 1800s.

Above: View along Littleworth Lane, Rossington, facing south.

Below: West End Lane, New Rossington, by Edgar Leonard Scrivens. The following excerpt is taken from the *Doncaster Gazette*, 1 August 1913:

Of the two types of houses, one has a frontage of over 20ft, and on the ground floor there is an entrance porch, a parlour measuring 15ft 9in. by 11ft, a kitchen 13ft 6in. by 11ft 9in., a scullery 7ft 6in. by 10ft 2in., a separate bathroom, with pantry, coal house and other offices. While on the first floor there are four bedrooms. The second type has a frontage of 14ft and contains a parlour, kitchen scullery, bathroom, coalhouse and three bedrooms. All the houses are built in a pleasant cottage-style, as at Maltby, and are faced with Armitage's pressed bricks and roofed with red tiles.

Above: New Rossington with the Royal Hotel on the right and the market on the left. The hotel has been a favourite watering hole for many generations of Rossington folk. Rossington resident May Shaw recalls the days when her husband, Ruben, and his dad used to put up the market stalls together for the traders: 'They would erect them on a Thursday and take them down on a Friday when the market had finished. The stalls were stored at the side of Billy Bell's (Billy the Fish) mother's house for years.' The Hippodrome was constructed adjacent to the Royal and Rossington acquired its own picture house. The pub has recently been demolished. The Hippodrome opened in 1929 and closed in 1962.

Below: The Circle, New Rossington, with King Avenue in the distance. The whole of the village was built by Messrs Hopkinson & Co. of Worksop, who completed the contract for the Maltby New Village after the failure of the original contractor. It is interesting to note that the houses offered a safe opening for the private investor. As the houses were built, they were offered for sale on the condition that they were leased to the Colliery Company for a term of years, the company thus guaranteeing the rent and also relieving the owner of the cost of repairs.

Station Road, Rossington, looking towards St Michael's church. Fountain Cottages are on the left.

GNR lads pose for the camera in Station Road, Rossington. Fountain Cottages are to the right and Ivy House Farm is to the rear. Mathew Henry Stiles, who operated as a photographer and had a business in French Gate, took the picture. Note that there is another photographer taking pictures in the background.

Aerial view of Tickhill taken from St Mary's church with St Mary's Road cutting through the picture. During the latter half of the nineteenth century, Tickhill was described as:

> A small ancient town and township, pleasantly situated in a fertile valley, through which runs a brook, which gives rise to the river Torne... It is the head of an extensive baronial liberty and contains 4,200 acres of land and had 1,915 inhabitants in 1861. The parish of Tickhill, which includes also the townships of Stancill-with-Wellingley and Wilsic, contains 5,400 acres and had 1,980 souls in 1861. The manorial rights and the castle, with about 651 acres of land, belong to the Crown, as part of the Duchy of Lancaster, and are leased to the Earl of Scarborough, besides whom there are several small freeholders. This large township contains many scattered farms, extending two miles round the town... The town is well built and the streets are neat and spacious. Gas works were established in 1860 by Mr Denton.

Doncaster Road, Tickhill, facing Wadworth.

Above: A view of West Gate with the castle in the distance, taken by Edgar Leonard Scrivens. Under the 1894 Local Government Act, Tickhill was given Urban District status. The first UDC meeting took place in January 1895. Nine councillors each held office for three years, after which time they sought re-election. They were all part-time officials. The UDC continued until 1974, when the new Doncaster Metropolitan District Council absorbed Tickhill.

Below: Sunderland Street looking toward the Buttercross. In his book, *Tickhill, Portrait of an English Country Town* (1995), Tom Beastall notes:

> In 1875 the UDC had laid sewers to the old sewerage works in Sunderland Street and began regular inspection of scavenging, nuisance removal, housing, shops, slaughterhouses and farm dairies. The medical officer of health visited the schools and gave advice to the UDC about middens, closets and wells. His advice led to the formation, in 1927, of the Doncaster-Tickhill water board to improve the supply of pure water to households. By 1931 a new sewage works had opened, capable of serving a population of 2,500.

Above: Castle Gate, looking south-west with the castle in the distance and the Red Lion on the right. Edgar Leonard Scrivens took this view before the library was built on the left in 1908.

Below: Sunderland Street, Tickhill, looking south. At the time this picture was taken (around 1905), the commercial people who occupied the street included a huckster, plumber, bricklayer, farmer, threshing-machine owner, hay dealer and butcher. The Tickhill Gas Light & Coke Co. manager, Herbert Hickson also lived on Sunderland Street.

Above: This photographic card shows Mr John Bee ('Phagee' Bee) the printer in his later years, taken in Tickhill Market Place outside the earlier shops of Messrs Jarvis, drapers and grocers. John Bee is the only printer to appear in any records relating to Tickhill in the nineteenth century – notably the 1851 and 1861 census returns. His name is listed in all the district directories of the period and on into the late 1890s. He was a good printer and poster writer. He was born in London and received his training in that city. He was a great man and the father of thirty-three children – the fruit of three marriages. When asked about his family, he would frequently say that he had had twice thirty-two children; for every infant that he had buried, his wife had had another later to make up the number of surviving children. He died on 1 January 1900, aged eighty-six years, at the home of his eldest son in Worksop.

Below: Sunderland Street looking towards the Buttercross.

Tickhill Market Place with Castle Gate and the Red Lion to the left and the business premises of George Jenkinson, grocer and draper, and William Burton, plumber, in the centre. St Mary's church is to the rear. The picture was taken prior to 1913 when a telegraph pole was erected outside the post office on the extreme left. In *The Homeland Handbooks: Doncaster and the Doncaster Area* (1925), it is mentioned that Tickhill's 'general air of antiquity is in marked contrast to the industrial complexion the [Doncaster] district is assuming by the opening of collieries'.

View from North Gate facing the Buttercross, with the new library in the distance. St Leonard's/Parish Rooms and the Three Crowns public house are on the left.

Maltby Road, Tickhill, with the rebuilt Traveller's Rest public house on the right. The rebuilding work for this establishment took place in 1908.

A view of Castle Gate, Tickhill, facing the Buttercross and taken by Epworth-based photographer J. Bottomley. Photographer George Crossland later occupied the premises on the right, where the men are standing in the doorway. The Red Lion public house may be seen on the left.

Above: Scene at Rolan Bridge, Tickhill, captured by local photographer George Crossland. This picture allegedly includes some of the Kimberley children.

Below: Children enjoying themselves near the Buttercross, Tickhill.

AIRING THE BABIES NEAR THE DAM AT TICKHILL

Tickhill photographer George Crossland has aptly titled this picture, 'Airing the babies near the dam at Tickhill'.

Soldiers passing along Sunderland Street, near Alderson Drive. Troops from the Scottish Horse and South Irish Horse stayed in Tickhill during the war, 1914-18. Forty Tickhill men lost their lives in the hostilities. T.W. Beastall (op. cit.) notes:

Tickhill had good stabling, grazing land, accommodation and a railway station, so it was not surprising that two cavalry regiments trained here. Soldiers slept in haylofts and granaries not in use... The Methodist schoolroom, the Millstone Hotel, the Carpenter's Arms, the Parish Room and the library were used as clubrooms for the troops.

Soldiers in Back Lane/St Mary's Road near the rear of the old Co-op. Baths were provided for the soldiers at the library during their stay in Tickhill.

Sunderland Street, Tickhill, featuring the business premises of general drapers and outfitters, Jarvis & Sons. Further along is the White Horse beerhouse, which closed in 1907.

Scene outside the house of builder R.H. Rawson in West Gate. Whether the gentleman posing is
Rawson himself is unknown. Adjacent is the property of painter and decorator, Mr Sam James.

An old carrier's cart driven by Isaac Newton, the owner. The boy was W.M. Milthorp; the original
version of this photograph must have been taken around 1873 or '74. The man pictured standing is said
to be George Beet (or 'Ratty' Beet, gravedigger for many years at the end of the nineteenth century).
The houses have now been converted to Foulstones antique shops, Castle Gate.

Above: During the last quarter of the nineteenth century, Wadworth was described as a 'considerable and well-built village... F.J.S. Foljambe, Esq. (Lord of the Manor), Francis Huntsman, Esq., Revd J.C. Ross and Mrs Hatfield are the principal owners'. In the 1960s and '70s, much redevelopment work took place; some may say for the better, others for the worse. Derelict properties in Wadworth are seen here before demolition in a view looking from the cricket field to High Street.

Below: A yard off Carr Lane, near Post Office Row, Wadworth. Note the new flats in the background.

Above: An agricultural scene, dating from around 1905, at Grange Farm, Carr Lane, Wadworth. It is understood that the water cart on the right was used to fetch water from Rossington for the steam engine. Note the ash box under the steam engine, placed there to prevent any stray cinders setting the straw alight.

Below: This view shows High Street, Wadworth, looking towards the cricket field, *c.* 1970. The entrance to the old Wesleyan Chapel may be seen on the right.

This row of cottages at Wadworth, taken from the yard of the White Hart public house, is called Ratten Row. Most of the area has since been redeveloped. Note the new flats off centre to the right. Much of the old stone property in Wadworth was cleared under several compulsory Purchase Orders. At the time it was stated by the Rural District Council that most of the houses concerned suffered badly from rising damp and poor sanitation. At a public enquiry, S.W. Wilson, representing two objectors, asked whether the RDC were using the order as an excuse for taking more land than they really needed to re-house the tenants of the village. Only fifty-three new units were required to do this, but the council was proposing to create ninety-nine, so that people from Loversall could be accommodated, he claimed.

Houses on Well Lane, Wadworth, that were cleared under the redevelopment scheme.

Church Lane, Wadworth, taken by Balby-based photographers James Simonton & Son. St Mary's church can be seen in the distance.

Another view by Simonton & Son shows Church View, Wadworth.

High Street, Wadworth, viewed from Wadworth Hill and looking towards the newly created Whitbeck Close. A number of the cottages depicted here were cleared in the Wadworth Clearance Orders, Nos 1, 2 and 3. Some details appeared in the *Doncaster Chronicle*, 25 April 1963:

Wadworth (No. 2) Clearance Order, 1963. Un-numbered cottages in High Street, Wadworth, occupied by Mrs A. Mitchell and Messrs J.A. Wortley, W.M. Porter, S. Jenkinson, H.R. Bates, E. Choppin, F. Lockwood and two further un-numbered cottages, High Street, now vacant. Together with the outbuildings and appurtenances to all the above-mentioned premises in the schedule. Dated this 25th day of April 1963. Signed: J. Meldrum, Clerk to the Council.

The cottages on the left have since been demolished.

High Street, Wadworth, with the church hall on the left, viewed from Main Street/Wadworth Hill. The property has since been converted to a private dwelling.

Above: Main Street, Wadworth, with the White Hart public house to the right. Note the fish and chip shop on Walnut Tree Hill, which formerly extended to Well Lane and Sweet Lane. The White Hart can be traced back to at least 1822.

Below: Well Lane, Wadworth, where much of the property depicted was cleared under the Demolition Orders.

Post Office Row, Wadworth, photographed by James Simonton & Son.

The yard of the cottage depicted above on Post Office Row is seen here, but has since been cleared.

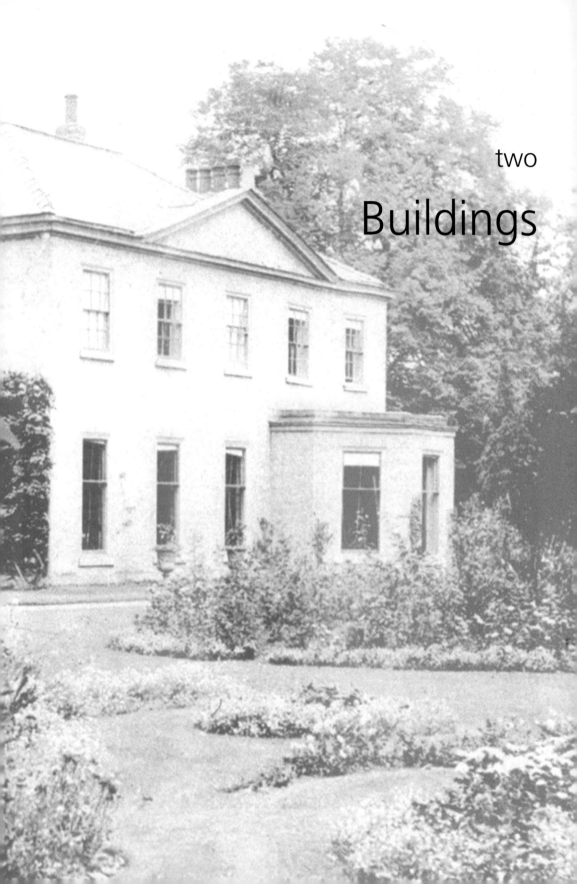

two

Buildings

An impressive building on Bawtry High Street, dating from between 1800 and 1810, that later became Sydney Barton's Café-de-Luxe and Garage.

45.10. Bawtry Hall. J.S.&S.

Parts of the present Bawtry Hall were built in 1779, following the sale of Bawtry Manor to Pemberton Milnes. Sections of an existing house may have been incorporated into this new building. Past residents include Bridget Pemberton Milnes with her second husband, Robert Monkton Arundel, 4th Viscount Galway and Major George H. Peake, who added a wing to the rear of the hall around 1905. The Peakes vacated the hall at the outbreak of the Second World War, moving to Sutton Hall, Thirsk. The West Kent Regiment occupied Bawtry Hall from 1939-1941 when it was taken over by the RAF and used as the headquarters of No. 1 (Bomber) Group. It is presently being used as a Christian conference centre.

Above: Premises on the south side of High Street, built 1800-1810. Formerly the Old House Hotel, the building is now Waddington's shop.

Below: Rossington Bridge House left, dating from around 1789, existed as an inn, the Corporation Arms, until 1850 when the license was revoked. It remained primarily a private house until returning to its former use in recent years when it became the Hare and Tortoise.

Rossington Hall was built around 1882 by R.J. Streatfield to the designs of W.M. Teulon on the site of an earlier house, 'Shooters Hill'. Some of its occupants were the Streatfield and Scarlett families. It was opened in 1952 as a special school, run by the Local Education Authority. During 1984, the South Yorkshire Apprentice Training School occupied the hall's stable block.

According to Frank Clarke, author of *Rossington: Glimpses into the Past* (1986), two schools appear to have existed in the village before the one depicted here: 'There is no doubt that a school existed in Rossington in 1652 when the Revd William Plaxton, Rector, left £6 13s 4d in his will to pay the salary of the schoolmaster and for the maintenance of a free school'. He also refers to an establishment in Littleworth Lane: 'The school was housed in the rectory on Littleworth Lane, where it remained, as far as is known, until the middle of the last century when it seems likely that James Brown gave the old school and schoolhouse next to the church'. The school is seen here before an extension was added in 1963.

Interior view of Rossington School during
the early 1960s.

Rossington Rectory was built in 1801 to William Lindley's designs for a schoolhouse. However, three
years later, Lindley altered his original plans and the building was converted for use as a rectory. It existed
in this form until 1979 when the Sheffield Diocese decided to sell it. Local businessman Ahmed Shah
purchased the property and his son, Nadeem, eventually converted it to a nursing home in 1987. An
extension was added in 1990 and the property sold in 1995, though it still thrives as a nursing home.

Sunderland House, Tickhill, also showing the entrance to Tickhill House (Alderson's) on the left of the picture. 'Castle Fields' is in the foreground – long before building began.

Tickhill Church of England Infants' School, Tithe Lane, converted from a Tithe barn, 1943-44. The school was demolished in 1969 and the remaining materials used to build a modern bungalow on the site in 1970. The schoolhouse was modernised in 1969 and converted into a modern dwelling house.

13. e Tickhill Castle. J.S.&S.

The Norman baron, Roger de Busli, built Tickhill Castle soon after the Conquest. Henry I probably added the gatehouse and Henry II the keep. The gatehouse is the principal part now standing. Several Kings stayed at Tickhill Castle and it suffered three sieges. Queen Eleanor, wife of Henry II founded a chapel within its walls and gave it the name of St Nicholas. After many vicissitudes, the castle endured its last siege during the Civil War. It was held for the king but surrendered after the Battle of Marston Moor. At the end of the conflict, the Earl of Manchester rode over to Tickhill to receive it. In his train rode a greater man than he – no other than Oliver Cromwell himself. The castle is now a fragmentary ruin. In the *Tickhill Castle Project* by Charles Hippisley-Cox, it is stated that:

> The house was probably built by the Hansby family towards the end of the sixteenth or early seventeenth century, re-using masonry from earlier dismantled buildings… This building was built against an earlier three-storey structure, with some of the mullion and transom windows being blocked in the process, remaining visible in what are now internal walls of the present house. The earlier building was probably less than a century old when the rest of the house was added. The front elevation has been substantially altered, yet the northern elevations retain some original features.

Lord Scarborough, from the nearby Sandbeck Park, opened Tickhill Library, Castle Gate on Wednesday 7 October 1908 at 3 p.m. The late Henry Shaw had made provisions in his will for the building, which was designed by P.N. Brundell. The firm of local Tickhill builders, R.H. Rawson & Sons, constructed the library.

WADWORTH HALL near DONCASTER.
Formerly the Seat of the
COPLEYS of WADWORTH.

Wadworth Hall is on the site of an earlier Elizabethan or Jacobean house, once occupied by the Copley family. The present hall was built about 1749 for the Wordsworth family, to the designs of renowned architect James Paine. In 1740-41, Paine had designed the interior decorations of Nostell Priory and in 1744 had won the commission for the Doncaster Mansion House. Mark Girouard, writing for *Country Life*, 1 September 1966, notes the following about the hall:

> Quite apart from whatever its stylistic significance may be, the unusual charm and distinction of Wadworth must strike even a casual visitor. It is all on a small scale, but of the greatest elegance. There is no park; the entry leads off a road on the edge of the village straight into the forecourt of the house... Inside, the house is divided up into simple rectangular rooms... the most ambitious internal feature is the staircase.

Following the death of Josias Wordsworth in 1780, his elder daughter, married to Sir Charles Kent Bart, inherited Wadworth. It was sold in 1823.

Above: Wadworth Hall was occupied by a number of individuals during the nineteenth and twentieth centuries, including J. Coulman Ross, Vicar of Loversall; W.A. Wayte, the well-known Doncaster dentist and G.E. Cooke Yarborough. After being purchased by the West Riding County Council in 1957, the hall was used as a welfare home for aged persons. This lasted until 1968, when the home was closed because of the high cost of maintenance and moved to a new building in Bentley. A year later, the hall – comprising 8.04 acres of land, a coach house and two lodges and described by the auctioneers, Shearman's, as a 'unique building' and 'a bit of old England' – was purchased by architects T.H. Johnson & Son. The RMA Partnership subsequently occupied the property.

Below: Wadworth Schools, which have a date stone, inscribed 1860.

4.9. The Vicarage. Wadworth. JS&S.

The *Doncaster Chronicle* of 6 October 1905 notes the following:

Wadworth's old vicarage has been razed to the ground and a much more suitable one built upon the site… It stands on the right hand of the hill and is situated close to the beautiful old church. The new building is at least 5ft higher than the old one and no pains have been spared in placing all the latest inventions to the front… It is interesting to note that during the time the workmen were engaged pulling down the old building, they came across a full-length skeleton not more than nine inches under the ground, which was remarkably well-preserved. This was not the only skeleton found, as no less than three large box-loads of them were removed into the church-yard and reverently buried… History tells us that the site of the vicarage is one of an old battleground and it is thought that the skeletons are those of some of the victims. Messrs Dennis Gill & Son started operations on the old vicarage on 10 April, and the new one, which does great credit to both builder and architect, was finished before the end of last month. The contract price for the work was £1, 667, which did not include the improvements to the outbuildings, and owing to these having received attention it is thought that nearer £2, 000 will be required… Mr J.D. Webster & Sons of Sheffield were the architects.

Situated south of Wadworth, Wilsic Hall probably dates from the period 1720-40. It is likely that it occupies the site of a smaller house, one of Tudor origin. Owners of the house have included the Tofield family, William Walker, the Barnsley Co-operative Society and, during the Second World War, Lt Griffith. The *Doncaster Chronicle* of 25 November 1948 reports a sale at the house: 'High prices were paid for carpets… good prices were also paid for paintings, including one of flowers and fruit, attributed to Baptiste, 88gns, a still life by Frans Snyder, 80gns'. On 11 December 1952, the *Don. Chron.* reported that Messrs Henry Spencer & Sons of Retford were selling the hall, although no bids had been received. It stood in 18 acres of wooded grounds and at that time was owned by A.P. Smith, a former director of British Ropes Ltd, who was emigrating to farm in Southern Rhodesia. During his occupation of the hall, he was charged at Leeds Assizes with making illegal alterations. On 28 August 1954, John James Dangerfield opened Wilsic as a country club. In February 1961 he was granted a license to sell by retail intoxicating liquors for consumption on or off the premises. He claimed that the club's membership was 740 and during the past year there had been 1,026 residential bookings.

three

Commerce

A group of commercial properties on Bawtry High Street, including Beckett's Bank and the post office. Before the railway was built, Bawtry's postal services had been centred on the Crown Inn. After the railway reached Bawtry, a post office was established in High Street and can be seen here. These premises have since been demolished; the site is now occupied by NatWest Bank.

Eric Ainley's grocers shop on Swan Street, Bawtry. Eric Ainley is seen in the Model T Ford. On the left is W.A. Wayte, the well-known Doncaster dentist, prior to starting his delivery rounds in and around the Bawtry district. The female depicted is Rosie Rossington.

Hepplewhite & Shaw's Garage in Bawtry. David Alick Edgar is third from the left under the petrol sign. David, who worked for the company for many years, was a Bawtry lad and lived in town at Cedar House on Doncaster Road. His family were well known, as his mother was the midwife and his father the local postman.

Barton's Garage in Market Place, Bawtry, which proudly announces the family, was Fordson dealers. The garage was housed in a building dating from 1691 and once occupied by the Dawson family. A Barton's salesman proudly poses on one of the company vehicles.

Above: Mrs Staveley's shop on Swan Street, Bawtry. Note the placard that reads: 'Man with broken back at the altar photographs'. Those depicted include Mr Franks, Mr Staveley (the lad) and Charlie Martin (a gravedigger).

Below: The premises of Bawtry Motor Co. on Doncaster Road, Bawtry. These buildings where owned by John T. Walker.

Above: Marshall's Garage (Bawtry) Ltd on South Parade, Bawtry. The site is now occupied by the China Rose restaurant. After twenty years' service to motorists, Marshall's Garage (Bawtry) opened their newest and most up-to-date filling station in South Parade, Bawtry in South Parade, Bawtry on Saturday 22 October 1966. And to mark the occasion, the firm made one of the Doncaster area's most inviting offers. They gave away a six-piece dining room suite to each of the first two motorists whose personal purchases of VIP petrol at the station reached a total of 100 gallons. Marshall's Garage was founded in 1946. Then Mr Marshall, who had recently left the RAF Bomber Command, took over with his brother a two-pump filling station in South Parade, Bawtry. It was this station, which was being replaced by the new premises. Contractors for the new building were T. &N. Stephenson and the architect was R.M. Bruce.

Below: Henderson's Garage, Rossington.

Above: Scene outside Rossington Co-op, where General William Bramwell Booth of the Salvation Army is addressing the crowd. The Co-op opened in 1915.

Below: The premises of J. Richardson's grocers and general dealers, Rossington.

Above: Sam James' house in West Gate where Mrs Harold Rawson's house now stands. Mrs James and Sarah can be seen by yard doors; Norah James and Sarah Brown squatting by house door and Miss 'Lizzie' Jenkinson by the window.

Below: Tickhill Garage was rebuilt in 1961 to blend in with the ancient charm of surrounding cottages in Castle Gate. The new garage was built on the site of the centuries-old building, which was demolished in May 1960. 'The difference is incomparable,' said Tony Preece, the proprietor, whose father, Maurice, founded the business in February 1919. He started at the existing site with a repair service and petrol station, selling petrol from cans only. In those days repairs were difficult because spare parts were almost non-existent and often had to be made by the repairer. Gradually accessories became more plentiful and the business developed so that in the following year, 1920, a Gilbert and Barker petrol pump was installed. It was one of the first kerb-side pumps in the district. This was followed by the acquisition of a Wolsey bus with solid tyres which was used as the first regular passenger service between Tickhill and Doncaster. The fare was 1s 3d single. A Model T Ford car was the next addition and then a taxi service was operated.

Above left: Lucy Frost's shop, Wadworth.

Above right: Lucy Frost's general store, Wadworth. The picture shows, from left to right: Mrs Lockwood, Mrs Massey (Frost) and Mrs Green.

George Jenkinson poses outside his store in Tickhill with the grocery department to the right and drapery to the left.

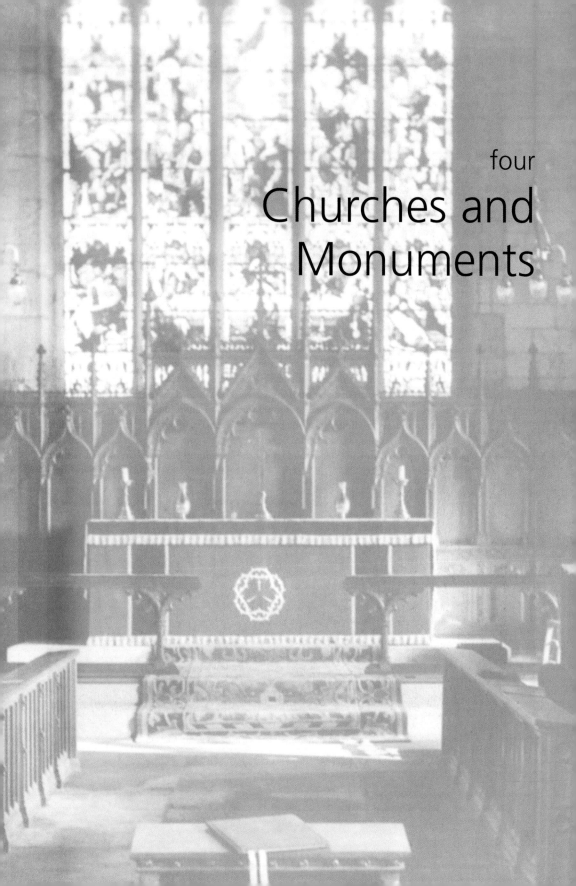

four
Churches and Monuments

St Nicholas's church, Bawtry began as a twelfth-century chapel of the Benedictine priory of Blyth. The early chapel was shorter and half as wide as the present church. Bawtry was a busy inland port with the wharf just below the church, making St Nicholas a natural patron. The church was partially rebuilt in 1686 and restored in 1833. It comprises nave with a clerestory on one side only, chancel, aisles, and a tower, which was added in 1712.

Interior view of St Nicholas's church, Bawtry.

Bawtry Market Cross, which was restored in the eighteenth century. A writer in a Sheffield newspaper of 1900 said: 'I noticed the cross was far decayed, weathered and wilfully mutilated at the base; that it was in danger of overbalancing and smashing to pieces at any moment. A tall, ugly single shaft, true – but neither antiquary nor native can afford to lose the end of it'.

St Michael's church, Rossington, c. 1827. This watercolour has been attributed to Roland Hibbard. The painting is one of thirty-seven watercolours of local ecclesiastical buildings and monuments painted by the artist and housed in Doncaster Museum and Art Gallery. Hibbard was born in Adwick-on-Dearne in 1777 and educated at University College, Oxford, where he was a pupil of Francis Nicholson of York. He lived in Handsworth, Sheffield until his death in 1841. Rossington parish church is of Norman foundation, with a Perpendicular tower. Rebuilt with the doorway and chancel arch incorporated, it contains a splendid old pulpit, carrying an inscription and traditionally believed to have been removed from Mary Magdalene's church at Doncaster. In the churchyard lies Charles Bosvile, known as 'King of the Gipsies,' who died in 1708 and hailed from Ravenfield, some ten miles to the west.

St Luke's church, Rossington. St Luke's church was built in 1916 to serve the new village as a daughter church to St Michael's. It became a parish and sister church in 1956. St Luke's was designed by FND Masters and built by C. Sprakes & Son of Doncaster. The Colliery Company provided a site for the church and the vicarage. Miss Annette Streatfield laid the foundation stone on 8 December 1915 and the Bishop of Sheffield dedicated the church on 18 October 1916.

Above: Tickhill Buttercross/Market Cross, in the centre of the small town, is a circular building of stone, erected in 1777. It consists of eight pillars, supporting a neat dome. Interestingly, a directory for 1871 states that, 'the Market, anciently held on Fridays, is now obsolete, but here is still an annual fair on the second Friday in October. The statutes or hirings for servants are held on the Friday after Martinmas Day'. T.W. Beastall in *Tickhill, Portrait of an English Country Town* (1995), adds that, 'the Market Cross [was] built by the Revd Christopher Alderson in 1777… It was said it provided shelter for the butter sellers in the market, hence its local name of Buttercross. William Lindley of Doncaster may have been the architect'.

Below: Tickhill Buttercross in a view looking towards Northgate. The old vicarage can be seen on the right.

E.L.S. 25-5. NORTHGATE, TICKHILL.

Above: St Mary's church is Tickhill's most beautiful ornament. Erected in the reign of Richard II, it is a fine specimen of church building for the larger parishes in the latter part of the fourteenth century. It is of early Perpendicular architecture and consists of nave with aisles and clerestory, chancel with side chapels, north and south porches and a lofty square tower. The west end opens to the nave and aisles by three elegant arches. The interior is very spacious, and contains two piscinae, an aumbry and numerous monuments both ancient and modern, among which are several tombs of merchants who lived in the fourteenth century. There is also a splendid tomb of alabaster, bearing effigies of Sir Richard Fitzwilliam and his lady, which was removed from the priory. The church was first lighted with gas in 1859. Several of the windows retain portions of ancient stained glass.

Below: Tickhill church interior showing the choir stalls and altar.

Above: West of Tickhill Castle in 1260 was an Augustinian Friary established by the Clarel family, living in Clarel Hall in Westgate. Tom Beastall (op. cit.) mentions that, 'John Clarel, chaplain to the Pope, granted the foundation to the Austin Friars in return for their intercession for the souls of himself and his family and that of Sir John Mancell, formerly treasurer of York'. By the fourteenth century, around twenty-four friars lived at the friary. Yet, by the dissolution of the monasteries in 1538, the numbers had waned to around eight. The present friary, according to John Magilton's *Archaeological Survey* (1977), is 'a former barn with a date stone of 1653 in the street gable end'. The house also contains a thirteenth-century lancet window and other masonry from the original friary.

Below: St Mary's church, Wadworth, is described as a spacious structure, comprising nave with aisles and clerestory, north and south porches and western tower. Some of its windows are of the Decorated and Perpendicular periods, while the south is of early Norman workmanship. The chancel was restored in 1865 and the nave in 1868, when the entire body of the church was fitted with open benches at an expense of upwards of £800, raised by voluntary subscriptions. The Higgins Chapel is at the east of the north aisle. It contains a piscine, sedilia for three priests, some fine specimens of ancient stained glass and several interesting altar tombs and other monuments. The register dates from 1575.

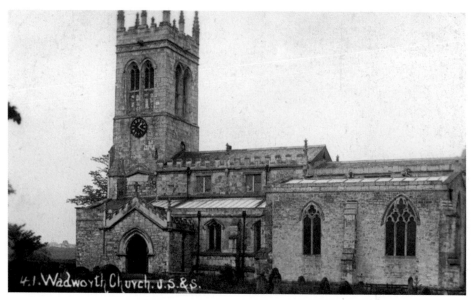

Left: Wadworth church interior showing the Fitzwilliam tomb.

Below: View of Wadworth Methodist Chapel, photographed by James Simonton & Son.

five

Events

Above: Individuals involved in the bicycle gymkhana at Bawtry Hall on 12 August 1908. The event was in support of the Bawtry and District Nursing Association.

Below: Bawtry Coronation Cycle Parade, 22 June 1911.

Garden fête at Bawtry Hall on 27 July 1910. The picture shows Lady Galway of Serlby Hall, in black and marked X, along with Bawtry Hall residents Mr and Mrs Peake who were judging the fancy dress cycle parade.

Meet of the Fitzwilliam Grove Hounds at Bawtry on Monday 15 March 1909, featuring Mr Peake of Bawtry Hall. The *Don. Chron.* of 19 March 1909 noted the following:

The meet at Bawtry on Monday was the prelude of good sport. Among the field were Mr R.C. Otter (who carried the horn), Lady Mabel Smith, Mr G.H. Aizlewood, Mr G.W. Chesterman, Mrs Chesterman, Captain Cook, Miss Denison, Mr H. Denison, Mr C. Darley, Lt-Col. Drake and officers R.H.A., Mr W.C. Easterfield, Mr G.B. Foster, Mr P.B. Foster, Mrs Foster, Mr J.B. Foster, Mr S. Haigh, Mr H. Hunt, Mr M.J. Hunter, Mr M.D. Holmes, Mrs Holmes, Captain Kent, Miss Otter, Mr H. Peake, Mrs Peake, Mr Harrison Smith, Mr R.J. Streatfield, Miss Streatfield, Miss Willey, Sir Archibald White, Mr D. Wright. These were driving: Mrs Otter, Miss Dorothy Otter, Mrs Shiffner and Misses Shiffner. Swinow Wood provided a fox and, with a good scent, hounds at once hustled him through the covert and ran very fast to the left of Martin Beck, through Dumplin Castle Plantation to Hesley Eleven Acres where the fugitive eluded pursuers, after a very fast fifteen minutes. From the ruins hounds hunted another fox nicely by the Nooking Flat, as if for Serlby Laurels, but, swinging thence right-handed, they ran through Whitewater Gorse to Toad Hole and were at fault thereabouts…

Scene from a hunt meet in Bawtry Market Place.

Soldiers in Bawtry Market Place during the First World War.

Soldiers and nurses on the platform at Bawtry's GNR station.

Another view of soldiers and nurses at Bawtry railway station. It is not clear whether they were on their way to or from Serlby Hall.

A scene in Bawtry
Market Place during
the First World War.

The King and Queen at Bawtry railway station during the September race meeting at Doncaster in 1948. The *Doncaster Chronicle* of 16 September 1948 recorded:

When the memories of other St Legers have faded the ones of 1948 must surely live on (writes Jocelyn). Every one of us who saw the King and Queen will perhaps cherish a favourite incident. Mine will always be of their Majesties' arrival at Bawtry when there was just a handful of us waiting on the station, and outside a group of grown ups and the local schoolchildren who had waved their flags while they waited, but who waved them with far greater vigour when the royal party arrived. I shall always remember the dismay on one of the women watchers who feared the railway staff might omit a covering for the slimy sleeper over the track where the King and Queen must cross the line. But just before the royal train drew into the station the staff attended to the task, and the watcher sighed with relief... When their Majesties left the royal train at Bawtry they were believed to be the first reigning sovereigns to have entered the station since 1904 when the late King Edward VII was a royal passenger... Presented to the King and Queen at Bawtry were Capt. H. Studdy (Chief Constable, West Riding Police), Mr F.V. Wagstaff (chairman, Bawtry Parish Council) and Mr F.S. Tann (stationmaster).

A crowd of Bawtry folk greet the King and Queen at Bawtry railway station.

Fancy dress parade at Bawtry.

Left: On Monday 10 June 1912, the first turf was cut in preparation for the sinking of Rossington Colliery. A large company was invited to witness the proceedings including mining magnates and officials high in the railway world. The new colliery was the joint enterprise of Sheepbridge Coal & Iron Co. and Messrs John Brown & Co. One man came from Southend-on-Sea the same morning as the ceremony and there were some who made the journey from London, Leeds, Hull, Grimsby, Goole and Sheffield.

Below: At the turf-cutting event, a crowd of sightseers and villagers were assembled, Union Jacks fluttered in the breeze, press photographers competed with one another for vantage points and everyone formed a circle around the spot where the pit shaft was to be. Nearby was a huge steam crane and suspended high, aloft in mid-air was a hoppit. In the centre of the circle stood Mrs Maurice Deacon (wife of the managing director of the Sheepbridge Coal & Iron Co.) and Lord Aberconway, formerly Sir Charles McLaren Bart, the chairman of Messrs John Brown & Co. His lordship handed Mrs Deacon a handsome silver spade. Mrs Deacon gracefully accepted and at once, cut the soil amid a hearty cheer.

Mrs Deacon Cutting The First Sod — Rossington Colliery. June 10.

Above: Soft as the ground was with the rain, the spade buckled in the process, but Mrs Deacon reversed it and succeeded in getting it perfectly straight again. Lord Aberconway thanked her for playing her part in the ceremony. The sun was shining and the interest shown by all those assembled in the work augured well for the future success of the undertaking. Later, more than 100 guests sat down for luncheon in the temporary colliery offices. It was anticipated that the Barnsley seam of coal would be reached at a depth of 800 to 850 yards and that something like three years would be occupied in preliminary work.

Below: The colliery was to be equipped on the most modern lines and a model village on the latest town-planning scheme was to be erected within a mile of the pithead. In a speech during the luncheon, Lord Aberconway said, 'we hope to build a mining village here, giving the men the very best conditions that modern science demands, and giving them all the advantages which workmen are entitled to as much as ourselves, and I feel that with good surroundings, institutes, churches and chapel, good schools and in the pleasant country district, we ought to attract the best type of collier that this world can provide and if we have the best type of collier to work our pits, I think we can feel our future is secured'.

Fifty Doncaster volunteers went into camp for the 1915 Whitsuntide holiday to learn something of the practical side of soldiering. They were members of the Doncaster Volunteer Training Corps, who had been drilling and route marching for the previous eight months. The camp was held in the grounds of Rossington Rectory by kind permission of the rector, Revd Nicholson, who placed his house and staff at the disposal of the corps. The camp cooking was done in his kitchen, the washing was done in his laundry and his stables and barns were converted into stores, armoury and sleeping quarters. The rectory lawn was the parade and drill ground, and a neighbouring field and woods were used for scouting and ambush work. For the villagers, the event was a sensation. The Union Jack fluttered from the church tower as armed sentries with bayonets paced to and fro before the rectory gates.

Scene outside Rossington Rectory during Whitsuntide, 1915.

Above: Meet of the Fitzwilliam (Grove) Hounds at Rossington, 11 November 1909. The meet has been photographed by Edgar Leonard Scrivens at the Station Road/Stripe Road junction. The site is now occupied by the Stirrup public house.

Below: Children are seen here posing in fancy dress on Gala Day in Rossington miners' welfare ground. At the rear is the bandstand.

Above: This scene from the time of the Second World War shows a shooting range behind Homescarr Wood, where members of the Rossington Home Guard are undergoing an inspection. The Rossington Home Guard unit was made up of miners along with Major E. Munson, the new village postmaster.

Below: Procession at Rossington where the banner reads: 'Don Valley Division, Rossington Labour Party, Women's Section, Founded 1926'.

Above: A procession at Rossington moving along Queen Mary's Road. In the background is Armstrong's shop, on the corner of the Grange Lane/Central Drive junction.

Below: Panoramic view of a procession in Sunderland Street, Tickhill – part of the 1911 Coronation celebrations.

Above: This picture was taken in Clarkson's Yard, Westgate, Tickhill, looking towards the back of Westfield House. In this 'hospital scene' – part of the 1911 Coronation celebrations – we can see, from left to right: Emmie Guest, Queenie and Edith Guest, Gwen Kimberley, Vernon and Fred Green.

Below: Pipe players at an event in Tickhill.

Folk participating in Tickhill's 1911 Coronation celebrations are seen here in Castle Gate with the new Co-op premises on right. The picture was taken before extensions to the store were completed in May 1913.

Navvies making the first line through Tickhill during 1906. N. Ellis notes in *South Yorkshire Railway Stations* (1994) that, 'coal was the incentive for constructing this belated railway [the South Yorkshire Joint Railway] which ran from Kirk Sandall to Dinnington, via Maltby to Dinnington, via Maltby and Tickhill, later called Tickhill and Wadworth'. Building the line seems to have progressed with few difficulties. Fred Kitchen, in his autobiography, *Brother to the Ox*, gives an account of the work of the navvies cutting this line, telling tales in graphic detail of drink, insanitary conditions, fighting, accidents and the civilising influence of the railway missionary. C.T. Goode (op. cit.) states that, 'construction of the South Yorkshire Joint Line was handed to a Leeds firm, Whittaker Bros, and was begun in the vicinity of the Dinnington Colliery sidings by the Rotherham Road Bridge in November 1905'. On 26 November 1909, a Board of Trade inspector made an official journey of inspection along the line from Barnby Dun to Laughton accompanied by the engineer and other representatives of the SYJR. Two Great Central locomotives of the heaviest type tested the bridges and viaduct.

Reconstruction of the Millstone, Tickhill, *c.* 1908. The work was carried out for Mappin's Masborough Old Brewery Ltd. Former licensees of the inn have included the following people: John Sidwell, W. Pearks, George Elliott, William Parkins, Francis Asher, Mrs Asher and G. Emerson.

Patriotic gathering at the Buttercross, Tickhill, as part of the 1917 Empire Day celebrations.

Flood scenes in Castle Gate, Tickhill, with North Gate in the distance, *c.* 1930.

Maltby Road, Tickhill, in the floods with a section of the South Yorkshire Joint Line in the distance.

Boys club parade at Tickhill. St Mary's Gate is to the right.

Opening of the sewage works in Paper Mill Lane, off Sunderland Street, Tickhill. Please see page 27 for Tom Beastall's account of this event.

Above: Peace celebrations at Tickhill's Buttercross, 19 July 1919. Note the 'Hang the Kaiser' slogan on the right.

Below: Tickhill relief distribution during a period of industrial unrest in the 1920s. The picture was taken in a yard looking towards the Red Lion in the distance.

Scene from a Tickhill show and sports day. The information on the dray informs spectators that it is from Laughton Road, Dinnington.

Hunt meet near the Buttercross, Tickhill.

Coronation celebrations in Sunderland Street, Tickhill, for King George VI and Queen Elizabeth, 1937.

Coronation celebrations at Tickhill, 1937.

Waiting for 'Tommy Atkins' (the name given to British soldiers), outside the post office with Castle Gate to the right.

A horse show at Wadworth with St Mary's church in the distance.

Wadworth garland makers are pictured during the May Day festivities, Friday 3 June 1927. Included in the picture are: Frank Slack, Mr Smith, Mr Tindall, Mr Needham, Mr Nelson, Mrs Marr, Mrs Hutchinson, Mrs Porter, Mrs Bell, Mrs Hanstock, Mrs Willoughby, Mrs Bee, Mrs Jenkinson, Sophia Hutchinson and Mrs Keeling.

Wadworth maypole with the White Hart Inn on the left, looking towards Tickhill.

Wadworth maypole celebrations are recalled quite interestingly in the *Doncaster Chronicle* of 3 May 1934:

The sun streams down on a perfect May Day of seventy years ago; and in ten cottages of this old village, ten pairs of hands are working. Let us go into one of these homes of Wadworth – into the home of Emmie Hutchinson. There, sitting at a corner of the table, surrounded by brightly coloured materials and flowers and holding in her hand a hoop of wire which is mysterious to the uninitiated, is a fair-haired ten-year-old girl. She is working swiftly and silently… An hour passes and yet another and the hoop and pretty-hued materials are assuming definite shape under Emma's nimble fingers. And soon – you will have guessed by now – a garland for the maypole has been completed… 29 May arrives. For days before – the ten garlands have been made two weeks ago – mothers, children, and even fathers have been busy preparing their holiday garb. The festivities have been spoken of in every house, in every inn for miles around. Small wonder then that on this day of joy making, the whole of the village is up very early. Crowds from village and town within a radius of many miles are hourly coming into Wadworth, until shortly before noon the place is filled… Now it's six o'clock. The crowd round the maypole parts and through the pathway that is made come ten or so young women or girls, each bearing the garland that is the work of their own hands. They each hand them to a young man who is standing at the side of the pole; he fixes them one by one to a rope and pulley, and they are sent to the top.

Wadworth maypole celebrations.

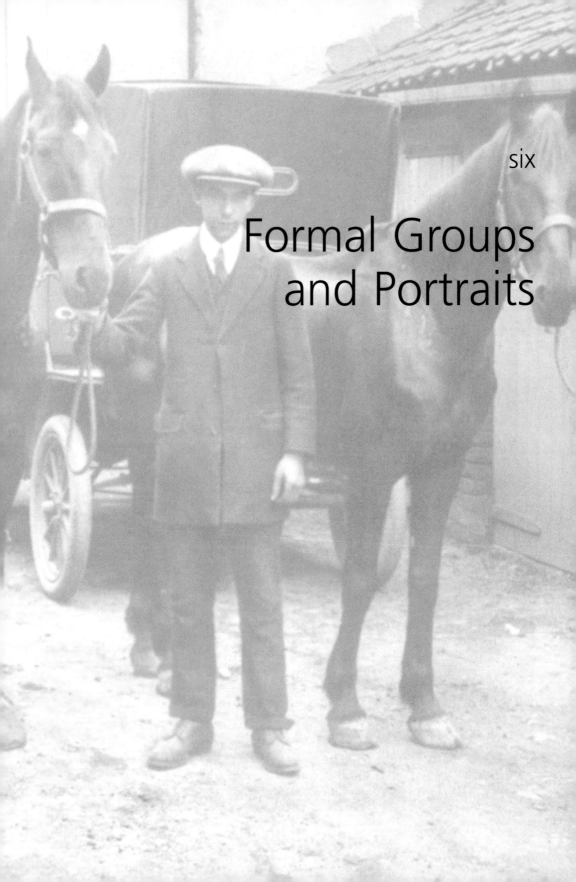

six

Formal Groups
and Portraits

Above: Bawtry cricket club. Philip Scowcroft in his book, *Cricket in Doncaster and District: An Outline History* (1985), notes: 'cricket locally has been played to village, church and country house backdrops, in parks and open spaces in Doncaster itself and in the shadow of colliery spoil heaps…[During the mid-nineteenth century] cricket continued to develop in the [Doncaster] villages…Bawtry [cricket club]…played on a beautiful ground in front of Bawtry Hall'.

Below: Members of Bawtry cricket club including: Jack Morris, John Shackleton, Jack Spencer, Mr Hall (umpire), George Jackson, Ted Bailey and Ron Williams.

Bawtry cricket club. Amongst those depicted are: Mr Hunt, Jack Peacock, Jack Warriner, Fred Lay, Jack Spencer, Jack Morris, George Jackson and Frank Wright.

Bawtry cricket club. Pictured are: Mr Lindley (umpire), Harold Watson, Ted Bailey, Les Tissington, Horace Bailey, Mr Crowcroft, Dewsnap, Ted Lindley and Ron Williams.

Group at Bawtry Hall.

Formal group at Bawtry.

96

Bawtry Home Guard in the goods yard at Bawtry station.

Local farmer Teddy Wilson (the man pictured wearing a hat, third from right with arms folded) poses with his potato picking workers in a field off Tickhill Road (near to his farm). The man in the truck is Tim Winters; Mollie Winters has also been identified, along with 'Old Man' Winters on the extreme right, wearing a flat cap.

Bawtry Shamrocks, whose home pitch was in a field opposite the Station Hotel in Station Road. Those identified include Tommy Shaw, Fred Hempsall, Ronnie Farminer and ? Mellors.

Rossington Colliery officials pictured during the 1926 strike. On the front row, from left to right: T. Clarkson, Stan Coe, H. Mettham, Sam Coe, J. Webster and H. Firth (ambulance man). Those identified on the back row, from left to right are: P. Pownall, A. Blount, F. Cusworth, S. Bradbury, T. Saxton, J. Leach, T. Webster, L. Lievesley and G. Wilkinson.

James Brown (junior), who died aged sixty-three on 19 April 1877. His obituary appears in the *Doncaster Gazette*, 27 April 1877:

> Nothing could have been more demonstrative of the esteem in which the late Mr James Brown was held than the gathering of the large multitude who assembled at Rossington on Tuesday afternoon last, to pay their last respects to the deceased gentleman's memory. All classes were largely represented, the aristocracy, magistracy, clergy, landed proprietors and tenantry, not only of the immediate neighbourhood, but for miles around, including also the district of Burton Leonard and Copgrove, another residence of the late Mr Brown near Knaresbro'. Doncaster, too, was largely interested, those present comprising the Mayor and several members of the Town Council, as well as a large number of the principal tradesmen of the borough.

Richard James Streatfield was born on 26 February 1844 and died on 30 July 1931. His obituary in the *Doncaster Gazette* of 1 August 1931, reads:

> Rossington Squire, death of R.J. Streatfield in Sussex, estate that formerly belonged to Doncaster Corporation. The Gazette regrets to announce that Mr R. J. Streatfield, the Squire of Rossington, died this (Thursday) morning at his Sussex home, 'The Rocks', Uckfield. He had been ill for a considerable time and had not been able to visit his Yorkshire estate for the last two years. He was a widower and leaves one daughter but no sons. Mr Streatfield inherited the Rossington estate from his uncle, the late Mr James Brown. Mr Richard James Streatfield was the only son of the late Mr Richard Shuttleworth Streatfield, JP, DL, High Sheriff of Sussex. His mother was, before her marriage, Charlotte Ann Brown, daughter of the late Mr James Bown of Rossington. He was born in 1844, and married in 1865, Miss Mary William Scarlett, eldest daughter of the late Mr James W. Scarlett, of Gighs, County Argyll. Mr Streatfield was a magistrate for Sussex and the West Riding of Yorkshire, and was formerly a lieutenant in the 5th Dragoon Guards and a captain in the Yorkshire Dragoons.

Above: Rossington Main Colliery Club committee. This photograph was taken in 1931.

Below: Members of Rossington Home Guard pose for the camera.

Members of the Rossington School football team are seen here in 1921. They include, from left to right, on the back row: S. McGann, T. Wren, T. Foster, D. Jarvis, -?-, G. Parker. Front row: L. Lievesley, J. Sims, W. Boden, T. Waker, H. Greenwood and ? Ward.

Rossington Boys' School, 1949/50.

Above: Fanny Cutler (at the horse's head and wife of Frank, pictured below) with children in the infants' schoolyard in Tithe Lane, Tickhill, June 1911. The children are taking part in a pageant to celebrate the Coronation of King George V and Queen Mary.

Below: Mr Frank Cutler with horse and dray, pictured with schoolchildren from Tickhill's Church of England Infants' School in the school playground, Tithe Lane in June 1911. This was one of the school's entries in the pageant to celebrate the Coronation of King George V and Queen Mary.

Tickhill cricket club. Scowcroft (op.cit.) mentions:

Other places…with active cricket teams by 1850 included Tickhill…The credit for forming, (or probably reforming, as a Tickhill team was active in 1845 and afterwards) Tickhill cricket club is given to the Revd Canon W. Bury, of Cambridge University and Nottinghamshire, in 'about 1860'. The club moved to its present ground early in the 1870s.

Tickhill cricketers pose for the camera.

Above: Members of Tickhill Band. T. Beastall (op.cit.) mentions: 'The British Legion and the Tickhill Jubilee Band were active in the years between 1918 and 1939'.

Below: Tickhill cricket club. T. Beastall (op.cit.) comments:

Support for [Tickhill] Cricket team brought people of different social backgrounds together…Cricket flourished after the war ended in 1918 [Tickhill had a team named the 'Thursday XI' as Thursday was half-day closing for Tickhill people]…[cricket] was first played [in Tickhill] on a site on Water Lane from the 1850s…In the early part of [the twentieth] century, four members of the White family of Leahurst were cricketers. One of these, Sir Archibald White, was captain of the Yorkshire XI from 1912 to 1914. In 1912 he brought the Yorkshire side to play at Tickhill.

Above: Pupils at the Dormer House School, Sunderland Street. Those depicted include: Wilf Sanders, the Whinfrey sisters, I. Guest, Jones, Gwen Kimberley, Guest, Noel Dixon, Emmy Guest, Sarah Brown, Cyril Brookfield, Dolly Sanders, Robin Hornshaw (teacher), Keith Dixon, Carl Dixon, John Henry Audus Kimberley and Hornshaw.

Below: Robert Saxton (left) with his son, Graham (centre), and groom (right). They are all pictured in Saxton's yard, Castle Gate, Tickhill, with Robert Saxton's Bay Hunter. In the background is a Model T Ford motor car.

Above: Pupils are pictured outside the schoolhouse at the Tickhill Infants' in Tithe Lane.

Below: Folk involved in a fancy dress dance inside Tickhill Library to commemorate the opening of the building in October 1908.

A proud moment for a Tickhill couple on the day of their wedding captured by Doncaster photographers Garrison & Deakin.

Soldiers posing in Tickhill.

Wadworth cricket team.

Wadworth cricket team, c. 1920 From left to right, back row: Bernard Parker, Bill Kay, Frank Mullins, ? Huzzard, ? Smith, Dick Kirby. Front row: Dearan ?, ? Elvidge, ? Moyser, Charlie Elvidge, Bill Huzzard, –?– and Frank Slack.

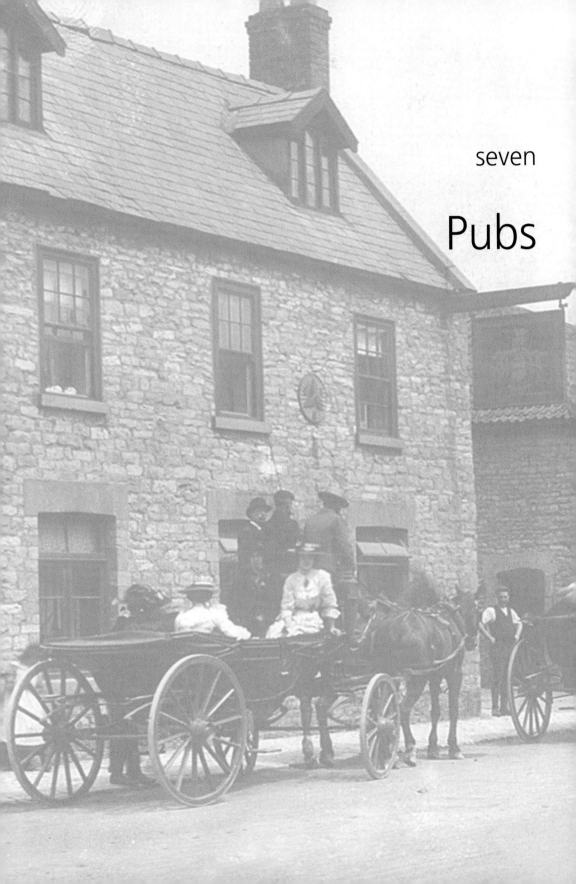

seven

Pubs

Above: The Crown Hotel, Bawtry. In January 1989, the notorious past of a Doncaster hotel was used as a tourist attraction. Trust house Forte Hotels hoped to cash in on highwayman Dick Turpin at the Crown Hotel and Posting House, Bawtry, tempting Americans to come to Doncaster to see the seventeenth-century inn from which he is supposed to have ridden. The Crown was featured in Trust house's 'Romance and Scandal' brochure, aimed at the American market. Dick Turpin was rumored to have stayed at the Crown on numerous occasions, riding out into the early morning mist as quickly as he had arrived under the cover of darkness. Numerous other rogues, villains and blackmailers were reputed to have followed in his footsteps and stayed at the Crown on their way to the scene of their misdeeds.

Below: The rebuilt Ship Inn, at the corner of Church Street/Gainsborough Road in Bawtry. Reconstruction work took place in 1908.

Above left: The rebuilt Station Hotel, Bawtry, after alterations in 1905. At the West Riding Magistrates Court on 9 January 1915, Edward Knowles, described as a traveling musician, appeared on the serious charge of trying to obtain information about the number of troops in the Bawtry district. Supt Minty explained that the alleged offence took place at Bawtry on 3 January. Thomas William Whittaker, a Bawtry labourer, stated that he occasionally acted as barman at the Station Hotel and was so employed on that date. The prisoner came in about 8 p.m. and was served with a glass of stout and some cigarettes. He pulled some papers out and began writing; then he began making enquiries in regard to the militia – what they had at Bawtry, how many soldiers and how many guns and whereabouts they were. Whittaker considered it was his duty to tell the customers not to give the prisoner the information. He then informed a quartermaster-sergeant. The military authorities, quite satisfied that he was gleaning information, detained the prisoner. At a subsequent court hearing there was a surprising sequel to the case, when it transpired that the prisoner was not a spy at all but of unsound mind. The police superintendent stated that the prisoner had once occupied a fair position in the musical world. He had some small private means and had once been in an asylum.

Above right: The Royal Hotel in Queen Mary's Road, Rossington. The coming of the colliers to the country villages around Doncaster during the early part of the last century brought the necessity of providing licensed houses with more accommodation than the ordinary village pub. One building firm which took advantage of this was Messrs Fredk Hopkinson & Co. (Worksop) Ltd. In 1921 the firm built the Royal Hotel at Rossington and a year later turned their attention to erecting one along similar lines at Stainforth. The King George Hotel, Church Road, Stainforth opened on Tuesday 5 December 1922. The hotel was not only built by Fredk Hopkinson but also designed by him. There was no formal opening ceremony at Stainforth, but J. Farnsworth, licensee of the Royal at Rossington, came over to represent the owner, Fredk Robinson, who was unable to be present, and H.N. Berry and J. Walker were present from Hatfield Main Colliery. The villagers were the guests of the owner at night. The first license-holder was Charles Edwin Lister, who served for eighteen years in the Royal Munster Fusiliers.

Demolition of the Royal Hotel, Rossington, March 2007.

Three Crowns, North Gate, Tickhill. This inn dates from at least 1822 and was renamed 'Buttercross'. However, while the outer walls of the inn – an old coaching house – were being renovated during 1926, the workmen discovered an ancient sign, which had been hidden for generations by an accumulation of plaster and dirt. It showed clearly that the hostelry had borne its sign for well over 200 years, the three crowns being plain to see, as well as the date, 1713. Past owners include Hannah Turnell and the Worksop & Retford Brewery Co. Ltd.

Above: Two Tickhill pubs are depicted here: the Millstone on the left and the Carpenter's Arms on the right. The Millstone can be traced back to at least 1822; the Carpenter's Arms to the same date.

Below: The Scarborough Arms, Sunderland Street, Tickhill. Records for the Scarborough Arms date back to at least 1838.

The Fox and Hounds, Main Street, Wadworth.

The White Hart Hotel, Main Street, Wadworth. At the West Riding Brewster Sessions held during February 1908, W.M. Gichard brought before the magistrates' notice plans of proposed extensions to the White Hart, which he said required separate dining rooms. There was, he argued, no opportunity for travellers to enjoy a meal there in privacy. They were obliged to take dinner in the common rooms. He gave figures showing that the demand for dinners was considerable. During September 1907, thirty meals were served in the first week, one hundred and twelve in the second (an exceptional week), thirty-five in the third, and twenty-nine in the fourth. Mrs Surr, the license-holder, gave evidence as to the desirability of increasing the dining and carriage accommodation. The application was granted.

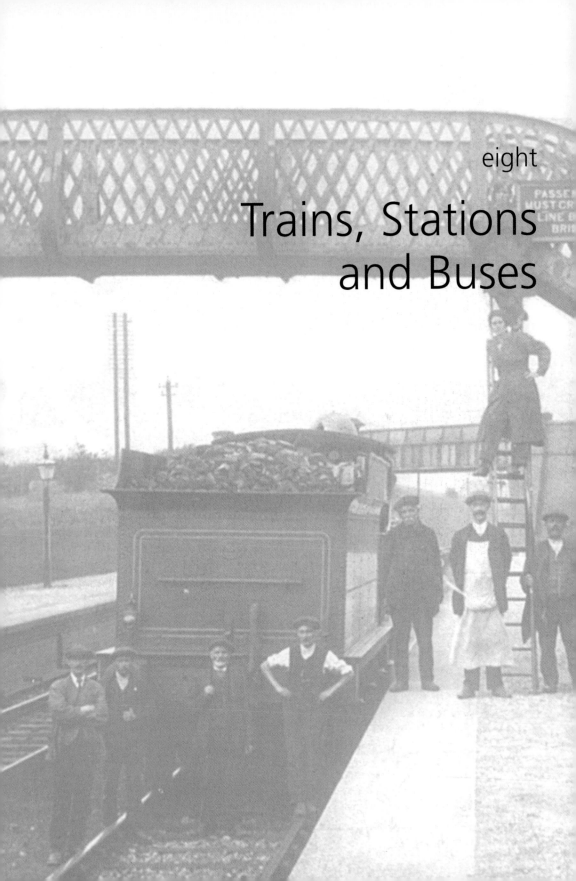

eight

Trains, Stations and Buses

Bawtry station was situated on the East Coast mainline of the GNR. In his book, *South Yorkshire Railway Stations* (1994), Norman Ellis comments on the individual style of Bawtry station's principal building, which 'was carried through to its chimney columns'. Note the long white-edged platforms and the wooden shelter featuring ecclesiastical window arches. According to Gerald Daniels and L.A. Dench in *Passengers No More* (1964) Bawtry station closed on 6 October 1958.

Gresley Class A3 Pacific locomotive 60059 *Tracery* passing through Bawtry station with a Leeds-King's Cross train on Sunday afternoon in August 1950. The train was photographed by Geoff Warnes. The locomotive was originally numbered 2558 (works No. 1614) when built as an A1 at Doncaster in March 1925. It was rebuilt as an A3 in July 1942, had a double chimney added in July 1958, trough deflectors fitted in September 1961 and was withdrawn in December 1962.

Wilfreda bus at Bawtry, pictured outside the premises of Hepplewhite & Shaw.

LNER locomotive No. 2561 passing through Rossington, which is four and a half miles south of Doncaster, just off the route of the old Great North Road. At one time it was closely identified with Doncaster, as the manor and the living were for several centuries owned by Doncaster Corporation. The village is on the railway mainline between King's Cross and Edinburgh. Named *Minoru*, the locomotive was built as an A1 at Doncaster in May 1925 with works No. 1617. It was rebuilt as an A3 in June 1944, became BR No. 60062 in July 1949, had a double chimney added in February 1959, trough deflectors fitted in July 1961, being withdrawn in December 1964.

Gresley A4 Pacific locomotive 60003 Andre K. McCosh at Rossington during the 1950s, photographed by Geoff Warnes. The locomotive was built at Doncaster as LNER No. 4494 and originally named *Osprey*.

Doncaster Corporation bus in King's Avenue, New Village, Rossington during the 1920s. Les Flint in his *Doncaster Corporation Transport Fleet Records, 1902-1974* (1973) notes that Doncaster Corporation first introduced motorbuses in 1922. These were Bristol 4 ton S/D motorbuses with Bristol B30D bodies, petrol engines and crash gear boxes.

Driver and conductor pose alongside an early Doncaster Corporation bus at Rossington. Doncaster Corporation first introduced double-decker buses in 1925.

Rossington bus negotiating the mainline level crossing, photographed by Don Temporal. The view is taken looking towards Doncaster.

Rossington Motors bus in the snow.

Rossington Motors bus moving along Station Road, Rossington, in the snow.

Doncaster Corporation bus No. 104 passes over the level crossings at Rossington during the 1950s. The house on the left is the only building that survives today. The view was taken looking towards the church.

View from the level crossings looking along Station Road, Rossington, photographed by James Simonton & Son.

Above: A horse and carriage belonging to the Saxtons is pictured here outside Tickhill station. Alfred Saxton's obituary, printed in the *Doncaster Gazette*, 15 April 1965, gives valuable information about the family business:

> He was a familiar figure in Tickhill for more than half a century and almost as well-known in Doncaster. He died at the house, 63 North Gate, where he was born seven years before Queen Victoria's Jubilee of 1887. To the generation that grew up after the First World War he will be at once associated with the business of carriers, cab proprietors and funeral furnishers which he inherited from his father, the late Mr Joseph Saxton and in which father and son together had more than 100 years' association with horses. The Saxtons once had a stable of fourteen horses and had twenty horse-drawn vehicles, among them waggonettes, landaus, victories, double-decker buses and two hearses. They were the first to operate a bus service from Tickhill with their eighteen-passenger double-decker vehicles, the fare to Doncaster being 1s, inside and 9d, outside. Saxton's patrons were not confined to the Doncaster run. His carriages were much in demand in the surrounding district particularly during Doncaster Race Week and it was no unusual thing for him to have as many as eight carriages and pairs at Sandbeck Hall at one time.

Below: Graham Saxton and friend pictured in Saxton's yard.

Above: Scene in Tickhill station, which was on a line constructed by the South Yorkshire Joint Railway, in an uneasy alliance formed by the North Eastern, the Lancashire and Yorkshire, the Great Central, the Midland and the Great Northern railways. Passenger trains on the South Yorkshire Joint Railway were initially operated by the GNR and GCR. But from October 1911 onwards, they were run solely by the latter. The station received passenger traffic for only nineteen years, but stayed open for goods trains until October 1964.

Below: The first passenger train in Tickhill station. The station was built in brick with a 350ft long platform, double tracking, waiting rooms and a stationmaster's house. An elegant ironwork bridge crossed the lines and a windmill water pump supplied water for the station, the house and the locomotives. It was first proposed to site the station for the cutting beyond Vineyard Cottage on Apy Hill Lane. Regular passenger services began in 1910. The line, however, had only had a minor influence on the town. Access to the station was by carrier's cart, bicycle or waggonette. Initially the passenger service met with some success but was unable to compete with the motor bus services, which were to link Doncaster with Worksop.

Railway staff posing in Tickhill station. Concerning rolling stock on the line SYJR, C.T. Goode (op. cit.) notes that, 'with five companies moving coal to and fro along its length, the South Yorkshire Joint Railway, which it must be remembered possessed neither locomotives nor rolling stock of its own, presented quite an interesting spectacle for much of its existence and the individual constituents were readily advertised, almost up to nationalisation, by their distinctive locomotives'.

Tickhill station looking in a sorry state in 1982.

Waiting for a train at Tickhill station. The Tickhill Methodist Sunday School, with an excursion to Cleethorpes one damp July day in 1910, was one of the first organisations to use the line. A party of 142 adults and 122 children booked tickets for a day at the seaside. In 1910 fares from Tickhill to Doncaster were 1s 8d first-class return and 1s third class. Joseph Saxton charged 2d to transport passengers to the station yard and paid the SYJR £1 a year for entry. On 21 March 1911, Wadworth Parish Council asked for Wadworth to be added to Tickhill in the station's name, 'in the interests of the public'.

Waiting for a train at Tickhill station. Disappointingly, by August 1911, the SYJR announced that receipts from passenger services were unsatisfactory. Services from that time were a little erratic. This led to reduced service; by 1915 there were only two passenger trains each way per day with an extra one on Saturdays. From 1917 to 1920, only Saturday services were run. An improvement took place in 1920 with two trains each way and three on Saturdays when there was a late evening train from Doncaster. Suspended during the General Strike of 1926, the passenger service was finally withdrawn in 1929. This was in spite of protestations by Lord Scarborough himself, who commented, '[I do] not suppose it was ever expected that this class of traffic would earn a profit to the railway. It was intended as a convenience to the public and public convenience cannot be left out of account'. In subsequent years only parcel, fish and excursion trains used the station.

Staff pose alongside their bus parked near the Buttercross at Tickhill. Beastall (op.cit.) notes:

A regular Retford-Harworth-Tickhill-Doncaster bus service was started by the Retford Motor Services Company which resulted in an 8d return fare to Doncaster after a fare cutting war [with another company operated by W.T. Underwood]. They became the East Midland Motor Services Company in 1927 and soon took over the Retford Company and linked Doncaster and Worksop via Tickhill with a half-hourly service with a Tickhill-Doncaster return fare of one shilling. This remained the standard provision for many years as the company earned a reputation for regularity and reliability.

WD Austerity 2-8-0 locomotive No. 900078 at Tickhill during the 1950s. Photographed by Geoff Warnes.

View of Rossington station looking north towards Doncaster. According to Gerald Daniels and
L.A. Dench (op.cit.) Rossington station closed on 6 October 1958 – the same day as Bawtry station
situated further south on the East Coast mainline.

A certain amount of military traffic was handled during the First World War, as can be seen here in
Tickhill station.

Other local titles published by Tempus

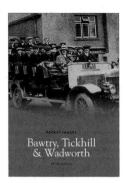

Bawtry, Tickhill & Wadworth
PETER TUFFREY

Bawtry, situated close to the Great North Road, was on the busy coach route north for many years, until the railways changed everything. This fascinating book, containing over 200 photographs, will appeal to all who know and love these bust commuter townships.

978 18458 8250 1

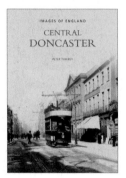

Central Doncaster
PETER TUFFREY

This collection of over 200 photographs of centre of Doncaster will fascinate all those who have ever lived or worked in the city. Many changes have occurred over the last century and this splendid sequence of images catalogues many of them beautifully.

978 07524 3016 4

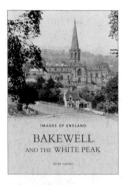

Bakewell and the White Peak
PETER TUFFREY

This selection of over 200 archive photographs offers a rare glimpse into Bakewell's past, from the turn of the nineteenth century over the subsequent 100 years. This book will appeal to anyone with an interest in the history of the town and the Derbyshire Peaks; whether they be a long-established resident or newcomer.

978 07524 3042 3

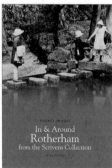

In and Around Rotherham
PETER TUFFREY

This fascinating collection of more than 180 old photographs traces some of the many ways in which Rotherham has changed over the last hundred years. A valuable historical record of life in the Yorkshire town, this book will reawaken nostalgic memories for many, while offering a unique glimpse of the past for others too young to have seen it for themselves.

978 18458 8174 0

If you are interested in purchasing other books published by Tempus, or in case you have difficulty finding any Tempus books in your local bookshop, you can also place orders directly through our website

www.tempus-publishing.com